PRESCHOOL

Illustrations by Michele Ackerman, Marie Allen, Martha Avilés, Tiphanie Beeke, Michelle Berg, Louise Gardner, Kallen Godsey, Thea Kliros, Kate Kolososki, Jane Maday, Michael Miller, Margie Moore, Robin Moro, Nicholas Myers, Ryan Sias, Peggy Tagel, George Ulrich, Ted Williams, David Wojtowycz, and Maria Woods

Photography by Art Explosion, Dreamstime, ImageClub, Jupiter Images Unlimited, PhotoDisc, Siede Preis Photography, Shutterstock, and Brian Warling Photography

Louis Weber, C.E.O.
Publications International, Ltd.
7373 North Cicero Avenue
Lincolnwood, Illinois 60712

Ground Floor, 59 Gloucester Place
London W1U 8JJ

Customer Service: 1-800-595-8484 or customer_service@pilbooks.com

www.pilbooks.com

p i kids is a trademark of Publications International, Ltd., and is registered in the United States.
Brain Games is a trademark of Publications International, Ltd.

8 7 6 5 4 3 2 1

Manufactured in China.

ISBN-10: 1-4508-3253-9
ISBN-13: 978-1-4508-3253-3

pi kids **publications international, ltd.**

Letter to Parents

Welcome to Brain Games!

Get ready for an exciting kind of early-learning activity! These 301 questions tackle key benchmarks across core categories such as language arts and math, as well as science, social sciences, physical and emotional development, fine arts, and foreign language. Categories are scattered throughout the book, and questions progress from easy to hard for a graduated learning experience. Colorful illustrations and photography help to present the material in a fun and engaging way. Answer keys for all questions are located in the last section of the book. Settle down, open the book, and have fun learning with your child today.

How to Use

- Open to the desired set of questions.

- Read the questions aloud. Ask your child to point to or name the answer.

- Answer keys are at the back of the book

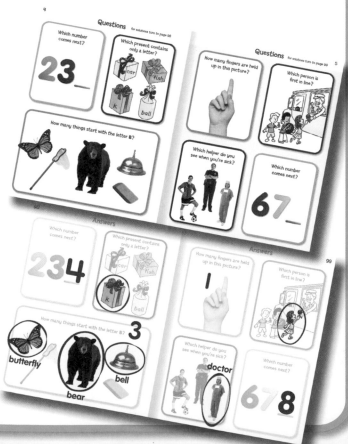

Some Tips

- Your child might not be familiar with all of the content on these pages. Take the time to introduce new concepts and characters when these kinds of questions come up.

- Encourage your child to use the book with friends and/or siblings, too. Take turns asking each other the questions. The material might serve as a good review for older children!

- Be positive and encouraging. Learning should be fun! When your child seems tired, frustrated, or unfocused, take a break. You can always play again later.

Questions

For solutions, turn to page 98.

Which number comes next?

23_

Which present contains only a letter?

car

fish

k

ball

How many things start with the letter B?

For solutions, turn to page 99.

Questions

How many fingers are held up in this picture?

Which person is first in line?

Which helper do you see when you're sick?

Which number comes next?

67_

Questions

For solutions, turn to page 100.

Which one means "good morning" in Spanish?

buenos días

buenas noches

Which instrument starts with the letter **P**?

Which letter comes next?

AB ___

Which letter comes next?

XY ___

Questions

Which monkey is in the middle?

Which helper puts out fires?

Which person is shorter?

Which toy costs more?

$9

$5

Questions

For solutions, turn to page 102.

How many things start with the letter **F**?

Which one do you see in spring?

How many things start with the letter **D**?

Questions

What is this picture?
What is its first letter?

_ar

Which one means "hello" in Spanish?

adiós

hola

What shape is the lollipop?

What kind of instrument is the girl playing?

Questions

For solutions, turn to page 104.

Which cat is smaller?

Which building is the tallest?

Which of these is a musical instrument?

Which animal is feeling sick?

Questions

Which snake is longer?

Are there more purple or green crayons?

How many fingers are held up in this picture?

Which of these objects begins with the letter K?

Questions

For solutions, turn to page 106.

Which number comes next?

45_

Which letter comes next?

Which letter comes next?

Which two pictures rhyme?

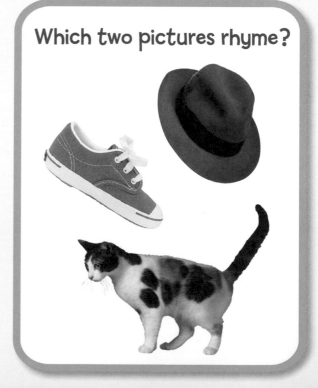

Questions

Do you see the letter **C** hidden 7 times in this picture?

Can you name each of the 7 objects?

How many blue things do you see?

Questions

For solutions, turn to page 108.

Which letter comes next?

Which two pictures rhyme?

How many yellow things do you see?

For solutions, turn to page 109.

Questions

Which of these objects begin with the letter **C**?

Is the bunny happy or angry?

How many black things do you see?

Questions

For solutions, turn to page 110.

Which toy costs more?

$3

$7

Which plate is full?

Which one means "good-bye" in Spanish?

hola

adiós

Which two pictures rhyme?

For solutions, turn to page 111.

Questions

**What is this picture?
What is its first letter?**

_at

**What is the
cat wearing?**

**How many fingers are held
up in this picture?**

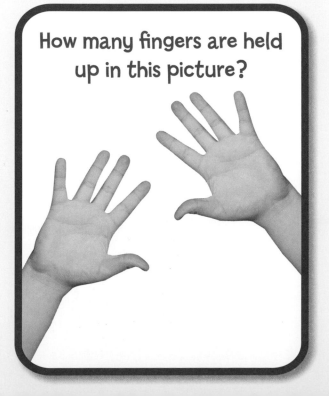

**What is this picture?
What is its first letter?**

_ift

Questions

For solutions, turn to page 112.

Which letter comes next?

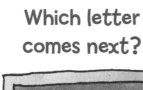

Is the puppy inside or outside the house?

What is this picture? What is its first letter?

_ree

What shape is the tent?

For solutions, turn to page 113.

Questions

Do you see the letter **D** hidden in the picture?

Which animal is slower?

How many orange things do you see?

Question

For solution, turn to page 114.

How many things in this picture start with the letter **T**?

For solutions, turn to page 115.

Questions

What season is it in this picture?

Do you see the letter **Z** hidden in the bowl of soup?

Which one of these is not an insect?

Which food starts with the letter **P**?

Questions

For solutions, turn to page 116.

How many things start with the letter H?

How many koalas do you see?

How many things start with the letter C?

For solutions, turn to page 117.

Questions

How many green things do you see?

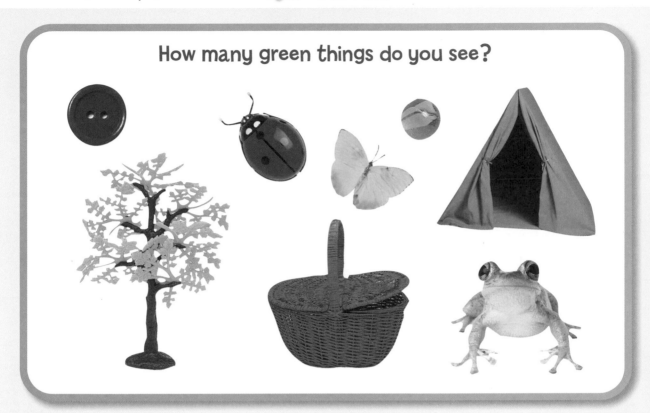

Are there more gorillas or goats?

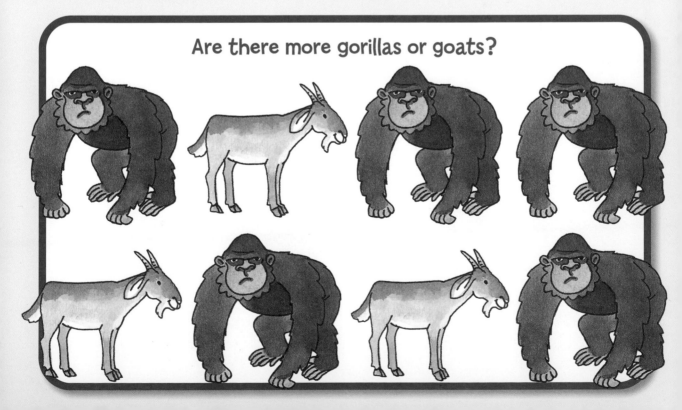

Questions

For solutions, turn to page 118.

What is the bear holding?

What is this picture? What is its first letter?

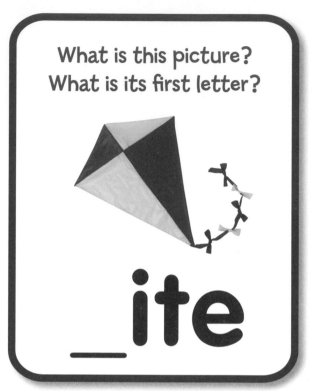

_ite

How many brown things do you see?

Questions

Which number comes next?

56_

Which one means "please" in Spanish?

el cerdo

por favor

Which two pictures rhyme?

Which box is closed?

Questions

For solutions, turn to page 120.

How many rockets do you see?

What is the correct order for these pictures?

For solutions, turn to page 121.

Questions

Which food starts with the letter I?

What is this picture? What is its first letter?

_ee

What shape is the badge?

Which two pictures rhyme?

Question

For solution, turn to page 122.

How many umbrellas can you find in this picture?

For solutions, turn to page 123.

Questions

Which animal purrs when it is happy?

Which bunny is in the hat?

Which car faces front?

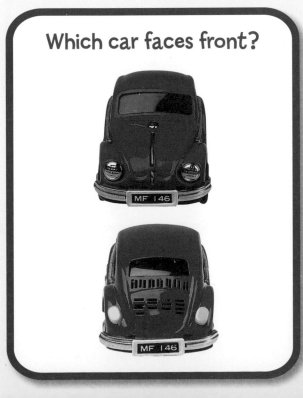

Which plant is the youngest?

Questions

For solutions, turn to page 124.

How many things start with the letter **G**?

Are there more zebras or buses?

How many things start with the letter **S**?

Do you see the letter **I** hidden 4 times in this picture?

How many red things do you see?

Questions

For solutions, turn to page 126.

Do you see the letter **T** hidden in the picture?

Which picture matches the word?

boat

Which animal is the opposite of small?

Which of these objects begins with the letter **A**?

Questions

For solutions, turn to page 127.

Which dog is the opposite of wet?

How many fingers are held up in this picture?

Are there more pumpkins or oranges?

Questions

For solutions, turn to page 128.

Which gift is on the left?

Which paint can is open?

Which number comes next?

78_

Which letter comes next?

Questions

Which two pictures rhyme?

Which bee is under the flower?

How many objects start with the letter **P**?

Questions

For solutions, turn to page 130.

How many apples are in the tree?

Which plate has more cookies?

Do you see the letter **B** hidden in this picture 3 times?

Questions

How many trucks are there?

Do you see the letter **P** hidden in this picture 4 times?

Questions

For solutions, turn to page 132.

How many bells
are there?

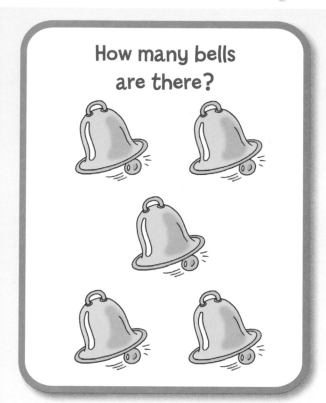

Which letter
comes next?

Do you see the letter **G**
hidden in this picture
2 times?

What is the correct first
letter for this word?

_tar

Questions

Which of these objects begin with the letter **L**?

What shape is the yo-yo?

Which picture matches the word?

hat

How many buttons can you find on the bear?

Questions

For solutions, turn to page 134.

Which letter comes next?

How many fingers are held up in this picture?

How many watermelon slices do you see?

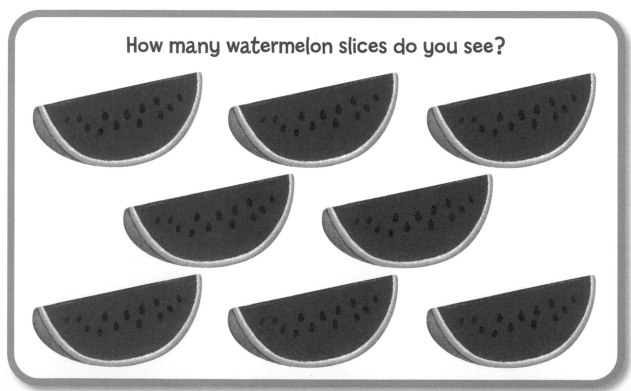

Questions

How many frogs are there?

Which of these objects begins with the letter **E**?

Which person keeps you and your neighborhood safe?

Which of these goes on your feet?

Questions

For solutions, turn to page 136.

How many birds are there?

How many things start with the letter **V**?

Questions

How many fingers does this person have?

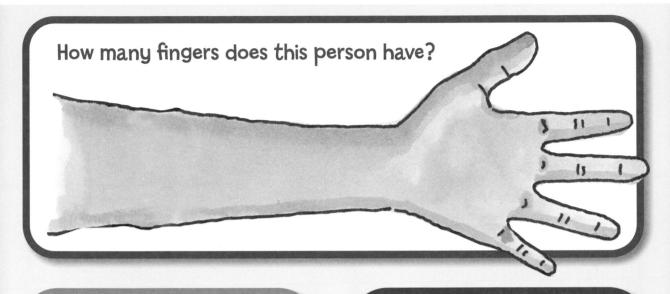

Which picture matches the word?

What shape is the door?

Questions

For solutions, turn to page 138.

Which two objects rhyme?

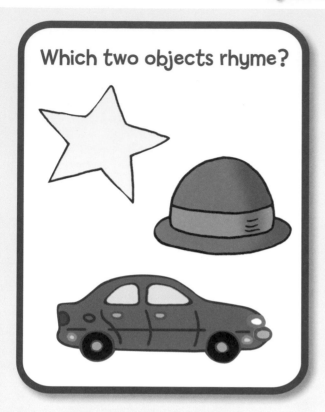

Which person is wearing glasses?

Which of these objects begin with the letter O?

Which letter comes next?

Do you see the letter **K** hidden in this picture 4 times?

Which animal says moo?

How many petals are on the flower?

Which of these objects begin with the letter **S**?

Questions

For solutions, turn to page 140.

How many squirrels do you see?

How many animals have four legs?

Do you see the letter **H** hidden in this picture 5 times?

Questions

Do you see the letter **R** hidden in this picture 3 times?

What two shapes are in the ice-cream cone?

How many birds are in the tree?

Which two objects rhyme?

Questions

For solutions, turn to page 142.

Which of these starts with the letter **W**?

How many fingers are held up in this picture?

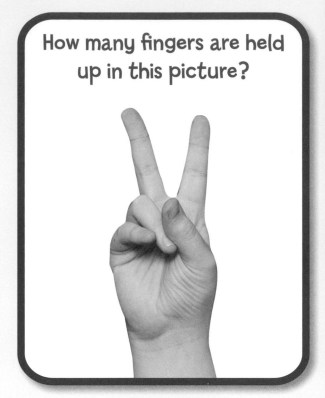

Which plane is above the cloud?

Is the cat crying or smiling?

Questions

Which side of the scale holds the heavier fruit?

Which of these objects begin with the letter **T**?

Which two animals rhyme?

How many tops are there?

Questions

For solutions, turn to page 144.

Which helper prepares food?

How many tigers are there?

Do you see the letter **Z** hidden in the picture 7 times?

Questions

How many helicopters are there?

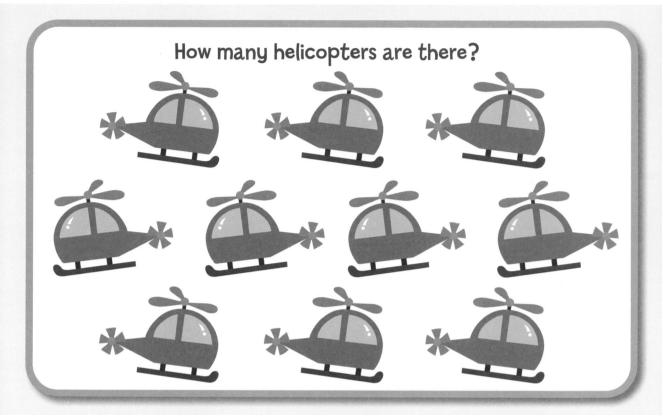

Which one is made from wool?

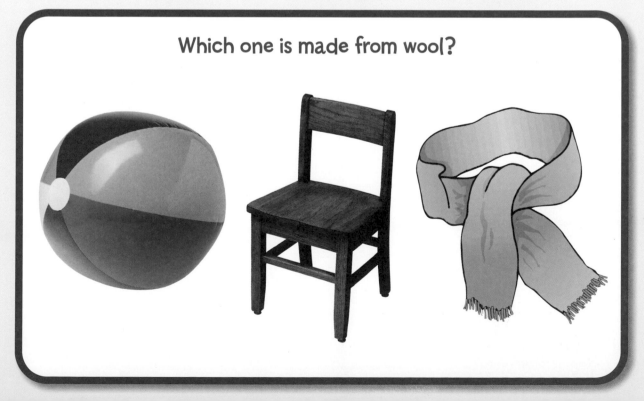

Questions

For solutions, turn to page 146.

Which one is the dog?

Which two objects rhyme?

Which picture matches the word?

jar

Which one will stick to the magnet?

Questions

How many objects start with the letter **J**?

What is the correct order for these pictures?

Questions

For solutions, turn to page 148.

Which person has blue eyes?

How many quails do you see?

Which person helps you find books?

Which two objects rhyme?

Do you see the letter **F** hidden in the picture 6 times?

Look at the candles. How old is Puppy?

How many circles can you find in this scene?

Which picture matches the word?

star

Question

For solution, turn to page 150.

Find all the things that start with the letter y.

For solutions, turn to page 151.

Questions

Do you see the letter S hidden in the picture 5 times?

Which animal lives in the nest?

How many animals have spots?

Questions

For solutions, turn to page 152.

Do you see the letter **W** hidden in the picture 4 times?

Which child is not following the rules?

Which animal is exactly the same as the one in the circle?

Questions

How many rectangles do you see in the house?

Which ball is the same as the one in the square?

Which picture matches the word?

sun

What color button comes next?

Questions

For solutions, turn to page 154.

Which sea creature's name starts the same way as "jack"?

Which picture matches the word?

truck

Which creature made this web?

Questions

For solutions, turn to page 155.

Which picture matches the word?

horse

Point to Earth.

Which of these is different?

How many monkeys are jumping on the bed?

Questions

For solutions, turn to page 156.

What color gift comes next?

Uh-oh! Hippo knocked the plant over. What should he say?

Thank you.

I'm sorry.

Which of these starts the same way as "bat"?

What is the correct first letter for this word?

_ish

How many red wagons are there?

Which picture matches the word?

lamb

Which animal can live in cold places?

Questions

For solutions, turn to page 158.

Which food should the rabbit eat?

What is the correct first letter for this word?

_og

Which one would you most likely see at Thanksgiving?

Which of these is different?

Questions

Which picture matches the word?

dinosaur

How many green trucks are there?

Which one would a baker wear?

What is the correct first letter for this word?

_ig

Questions

For solutions, turn to page 160.

Which one means "friend" in Spanish?

amigo

el gato

Which word starts the same way as "door"?

Find the things that start with the letter **R**.

Questions

For solutions, turn to page 161.

Which picture starts the same way as "sun"?

Point to the American flag.

Which of these goes with the brush in the circle?

Questions

For solutions, turn to page 162.

Which picture starts the same way as "egg"?

What do you brush before you go to bed?

Do you see the letter X hidden in the picture 5 times?

Which one means "stop"?

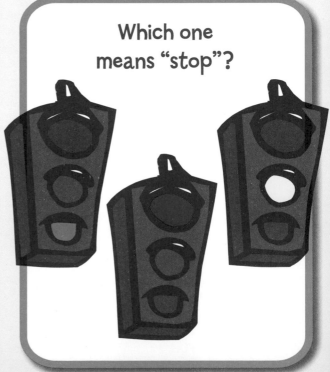

Which word starts the same way as "rock"?

Find all the things that start with the letter **W**.

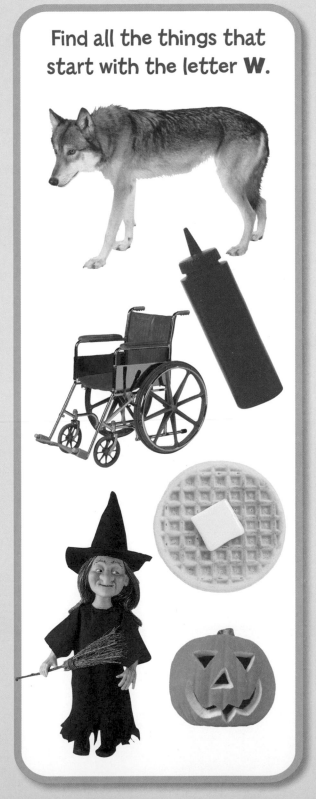

Question

For solution, turn to page 164.

How many yellow dogs are there?

For solutions, turn to page 165.

Questions

Is the hat on or off the dog's head?

In this line, who is the closest to the teacher?

What's wrong with this picture?

Questions

For solutions, turn to page 166.

Which drink is cold?

Which letter is a vowel?

Z

N **E**

Which one do you see at night?

Which one means "thank you" in Spanish?

gracias

adiós

Questions

Point to the part of the face you use to smell.

Which ball is the big one?

Find all the things that start with the letter **L**.

Questions

For solutions, turn to page 168.

How many squares are there?

What is the duck riding?

Which person is a girl?

Which thing starts the same way as "nut"?

Questions

What is the clown wearing on his head?

Which thing starts the same way as "igloo"?

How many diamonds are there?

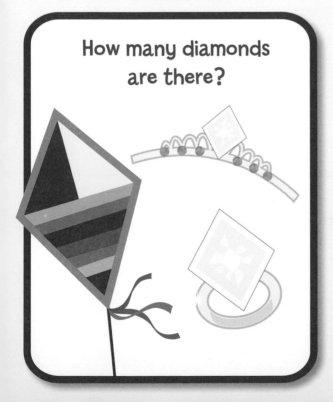

Which animal has horns?

Questions

For solutions, turn to page 170.

Which animal lives here?

Find all the things that start with the letter **S**.

For solutions, turn to page 171.

Questions

What's sitting on the dog?

How many yellow stars are in the sky?

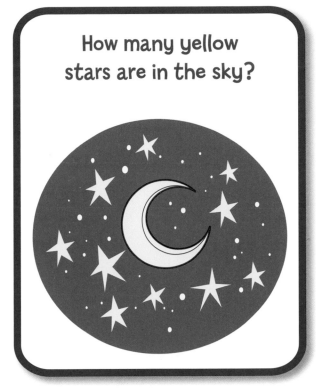

These letters are all mixed up! Point to the letters in each set in the correct order.

Questions

For solutions, turn to page 172.

What is the correct order for these pictures?

What animal is in the boat?

alligator
goat
cat

Which of these is different?

Questions

Which person is jumping the rope?

Point to the part of the face you use to taste.

What color bead comes next on the necklace?

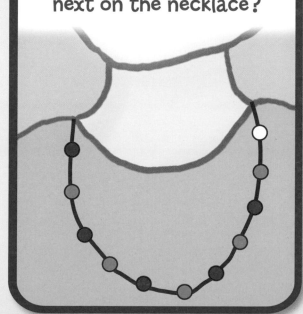

Which one is the farmer?

Questions

For solutions, turn to page 174.

What kind of weather do you need an umbrella for?

Which group of coins is equal to the exact price?

Questions

Point to the easel.

Which of these is exactly the same as the top crayon?

How many vehicles have four wheels?

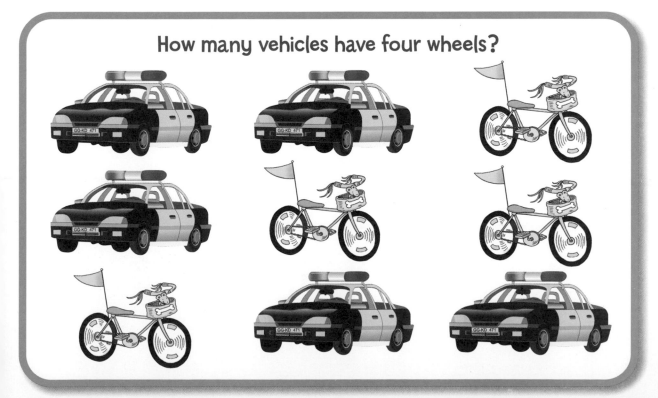

Questions

For solutions, turn to page 176.

Which is the oldest?

Which picture matches the word?

frog

Which bowl is the opposite of full?

For solutions, turn to page 177.

Questions

How many candles have stripes?

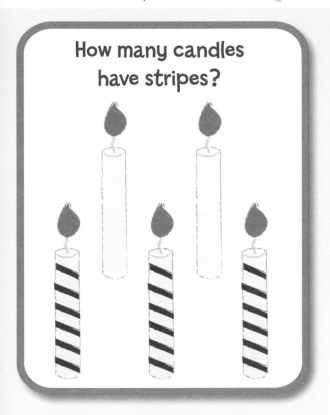

Which one is Little Miss Muffet?

What do you call a group of people who are all related? Here's a hint: It starts with the letter **F**.

Which one is floating?

Questions

For solutions, turn to page 178.

Find the word "stop" in this picture.

How many of these foods are fruits?

Question

How many roller coaster cars are yellow?

Questions

For solutions, turn to page 180.

Which letter is a consonant?

U V
E

Are there more orange or pink dinosaurs?

Which person is the mother?

How many dimes are there?

Questions

Are there more ducks or ducklings?

How many apples are red?

Which two things go together?

What do you say when someone gives you a present?

Questions

For solutions, turn to page 182.

What numbers would you dial in an emergency?

Which would you use to dance?

Which animal is upside down?

Questions

Which fruit has two sides that are almost exactly alike?

What is the correct order for these pictures?

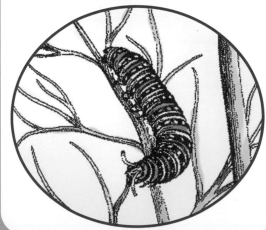

Questions

For solutions, turn to page 184.

Which one means "good night" in Spanish?

 **buenas noches**

estrella

Who sat on a wall and had a great fall?

Which two things go together?

Questions

What is the correct order for these pictures?

Which one is on the bottom?

Which person is the son?

Questions

For solutions, turn to page 186.

Find the word "go" in the picture.

Point to the bin you'd use to recycle this plastic bottle.

Look out the window. Is the weather rainy, sunny, or snowy?

What do you think the mouse is doing?

For solutions, turn to page 187.

Questions

How many shirts have polka dots?

Who lives in the igloo?

Who is oldest?

Which children are skipping?

Questions

For solutions, turn to page 188.

What is the correct order for these pictures?

Point to the chopsticks.

Which group of coins is equal to the exact price?

11¢

Point to the mouse.

How many things are hot?

Which two things go together?

What do you wash after using the bathroom?

Questions

For solutions, turn to page 190.

Find the word "ice" in this picture.

What do you say when you politely ask for something?

Give me
_____
Please

How many nickels are there?

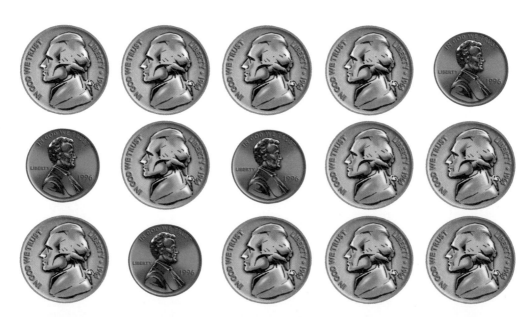

Questions

What kind of animal is hiding on the tree branch?

Find the word "bus" in this picture.

How many pennies are there?

What does a helmet protect?

Answers for page 4

Which number comes next?

2 3 4

Which present contains only a letter?

car

fish

k

ball

How many things start with the letter B?

3

butterfly

bear

bell

How many fingers are held up in this picture?

l

Which person is first in line?

Which helper do you see when you're sick?

doctor

Which number comes next?

6 7 **8**

Answers for page 6

Which one means
"good morning"
in Spanish?

buenos
días

buenas
noches

Which instrument starts
with the letter **P**?

piano

Which letter
comes next?

Which letter
comes next?

Which monkey is in the middle?

Which helper puts out fires?

firefighter

Which person is shorter?

Which toy costs more?

Answers for page 8

How many things start with the letter **F**?

3

fork   **flag**   **feather**

Which one do you see in spring?

flower

How many things start with the letter **D**?

2

dog   **doughnut**

What is this picture?
What is its first letter?

car

Which one means "hello" in Spanish?

adiós

hola

What shape is the lollipop?

heart

What kind of instrument is the girl playing?

guitar

Answers for page 10

Which cat is smaller?

Which building is the tallest?

Which of these is a musical instrument?

drum

Which animal is feeling sick?

Which snake is longer?

Are there more purple or green crayons?

How many fingers are held up in this picture?

1 2 3 4 6 7 8 5

8

Which of these objects begins with the letter K?

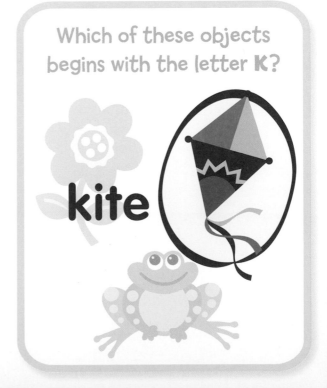

kite

Answers for page 12

Which number
comes next?

4 5 6

Which letter
comes next?

I J **K**

Which letter
comes next?

C D **E**

Which two pictures rhyme?

hat

cat

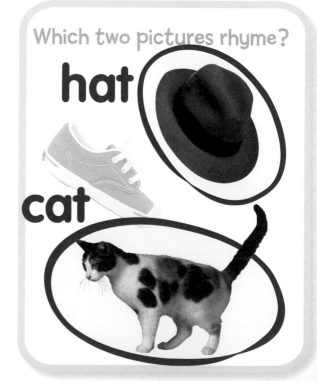

clock

curtain

c

c cat

cookie

c

cup

cake

c

carrot

Do you see the letter **C** hidden 7 times in this picture?

Can you name each of the 7 objects?

How many blue things do you see?

5

Answers for page 14

Which letter comes next?

Which two pictures rhyme?

box

fox

How many yellow things do you see?

5

Answers for page 15

Which of these objects begin with the letter **C**?

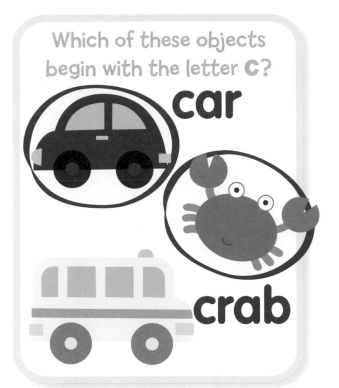

car

crab

Is the bunny happy or **angry**?

How many black things do you see?

6

Answers for page 16

Which toy costs more?

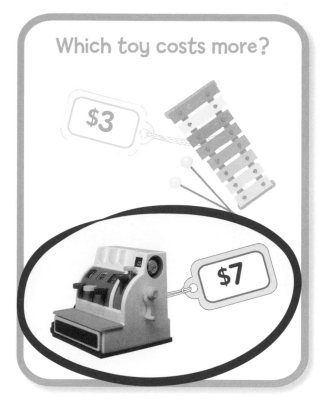

$3

$7

Which plate is full?

Which one means "good-bye" in Spanish?

hola

adiós

Which two pictures rhyme?

bee

tree

What is this picture?
What is its first letter?

What is the
cat wearing?

How many fingers are held
up in this picture?

What is this picture?
What is its first letter?

Which letter comes next?

Is the puppy (inside) or outside the house?

What is this picture?
What is its first letter?

tree

What shape is the tent?

triangle

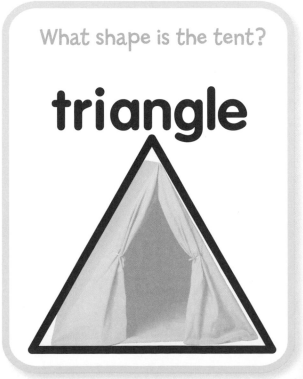

Do you see the letter **D** hidden in the picture?

Which animal is slower?

turtle

How many orange things do you see?

6

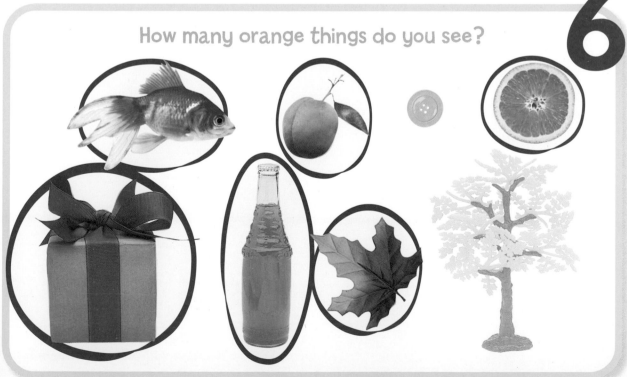

Answer for page 20

How many things in this picture start with the letter **T**?

turtle

5

tree

teacher

table

truck

What season is it in this picture?

winter

Do you see the letter **Z** hidden in the bowl of soup?

Which one of these is not an insect?

flamingo

Which food starts with the letter **P**?

pear

Answers for page 22

How many things start with the letter H?

3

hammer   heart   **hot dog**

How many koalas do you see?

3

How many things start with the letter C?

castle   **carrot**

2

4

How many green things do you see?

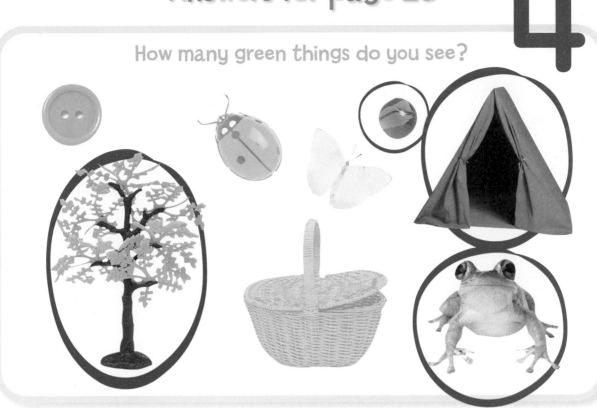

Are there more **gorillas** or goats?

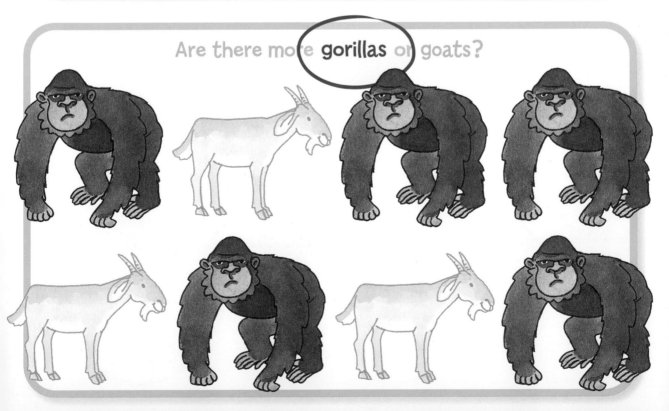

Answers for page 24

What is the
bear holding?

pear

What is this picture?
What is its first letter?

kite

How many brown things do you see?

7

Which number comes next?

5 6 **7**

Which one means "please" in Spanish?

el cerdo

por favor

Which two pictures rhyme?

duck
truck

Which box is closed?

Answers for page 26

How many rockets
do you see?

5

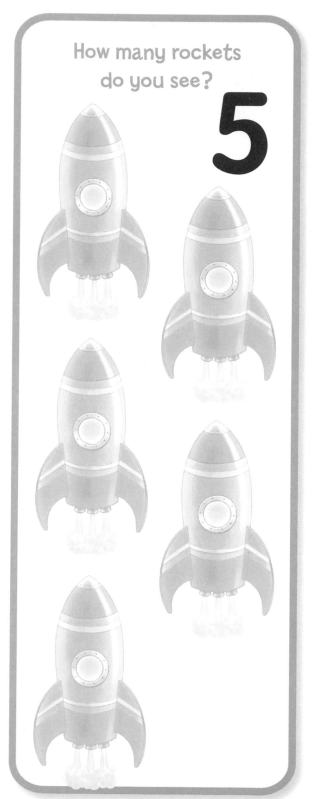

What is the correct order
for these pictures?

3

2

1

Which food starts
with the letter **I**?

ice
cream

What is this picture?
What is its first letter?

bee

What shape is
the badge?

star

Which objects rhyme?

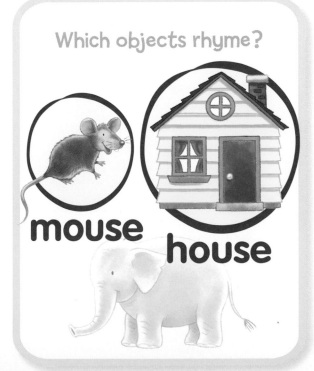

mouse

house

Answer for page 28

How many umbrellas can you find in this picture?

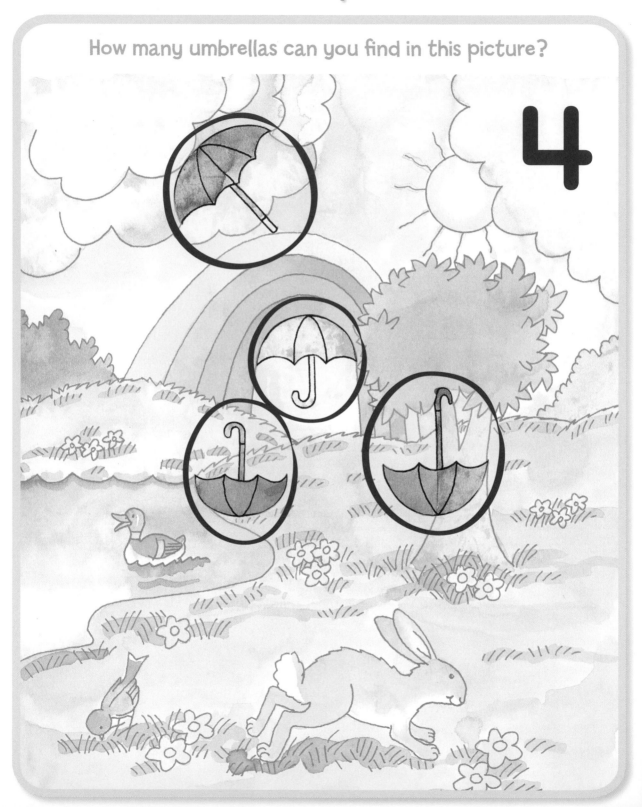

Which animal purrs when it is happy?

cat

Which bunny is in the hat?

Which car faces front?

Which plant is the youngest?

Answers for page 30

2

How many things start with the letter **G**?

glasses **grapes**

Are there more zebras or (**buses?**)

3

How many things start with the letter **S**?

starfish **spider** **spoon**

Do you see the letter **I** hidden 4 times in this picture?

How many red things do you see?

7

Answers for page 32

Do you see the letter **T** hidden in the picture?

Which picture matches the word?

boat

Which animal is the opposite of small?

big

Which of these objects begins with the letter **A**?

apple

Which dog is the opposite of wet?

dry

How many fingers are held up in this picture?

3   1   2   3

Are there more pumpkins or **oranges**?

Answers for page 34

Which gift is on the left?

Which paint can is open?

Which number comes next?

7 8 9

Which letter comes next?

Which two pictures rhyme?

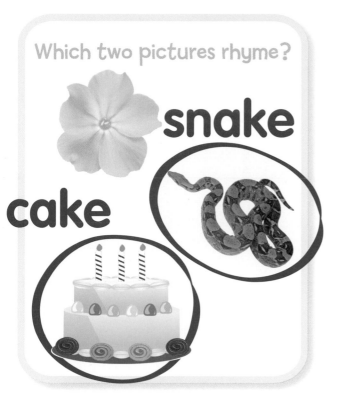

snake

cake

Which bee is under the flower?

How many objects start with the letter **P**?

3

panda

penguin

pumpkin

Answers for page 36

How many apples are in the tree?

5

Which plate has more cookies?

4

3

Do you see the letter **B** hidden in this picture 3 times?

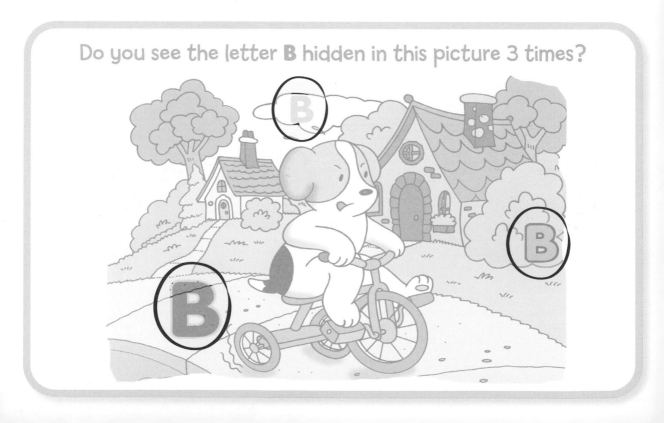

How many trucks are there?

9

Do you see the letter **P** hidden in this picture 4 times?

Answers for page 38

How many bells
are there?

5

Which letter
comes next?

Do you see the letter **G**
hidden in this picture
2 times?

What is the correct first
letter for this word?

<u>s</u>tar

Which of these objects begin with the letter **L**?

leaf

lion

What shape is the yo-yo?

circle

Which picture matches the word?

hat

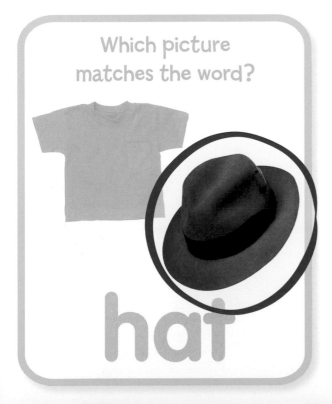

How many buttons can you find on the bear?

3

Answers for page 40

Which letter comes next?

How many fingers are held up in this picture?

How many watermelon slices do you see?

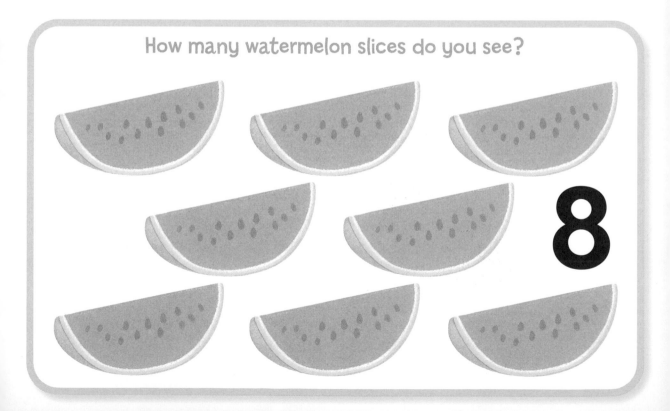

How many frogs
are there?

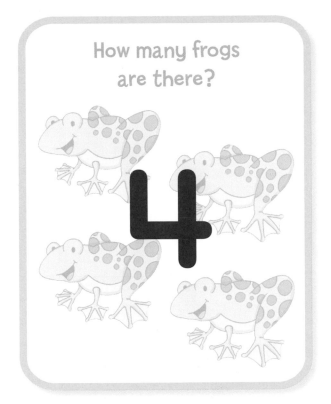

Which of these objects
begins with the letter **E**?

elephant

Which person
keeps you and your
neighborhood safe?

police officer

Which of these goes on
your feet?

socks

Answers for page 42

How many birds
are there?

3

How many things start
with the letter **V**?

3

violin

vase

van

How many fingers does this person have?

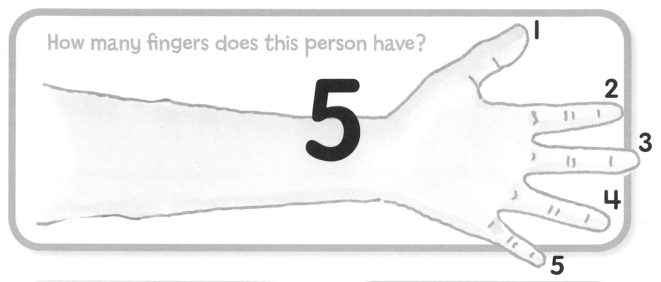

5

1
2
3
4
5

Which picture matches the word?

walrus

What shape is the door?

rectangle

Answers for page 44

Which two objects rhyme?

star

car

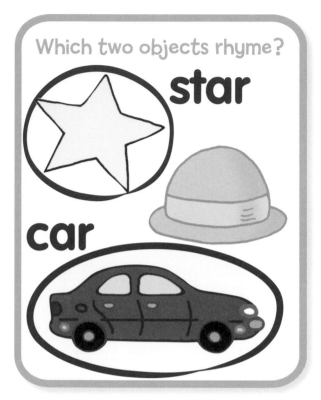

Which person is wearing glasses?

Which of these objects begin with the letter **o**?

owl

octopus

Which letter comes next?

EF**G**

Do you see the letter **K** hidden in this picture 4 times?

Which animal says moo?
COW

How many petals are on the flower?

8

Which of these objects begin with the letter S?

shoe

snake

Answers for page 46

How many squirrels do you see?

6

How many animals have four legs?

3

Do you see the letter **H** hidden in this picture 5 times?

Do you see the letter **R** hidden in this picture 3 times?

What two shapes are in the ice-cream cone?

circle

triangle

How many birds are in the tree?

6

Which two objects rhyme?

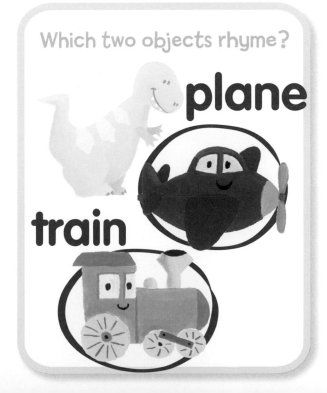

plane

train

Answers for page 48

Which of these starts
with the letter **W**?

whale

How many fingers are held
up in this picture?

Which plane is above the cloud?

Is the cat **crying**
or smiling?

Which side of the scale holds the heavier fruit?

right

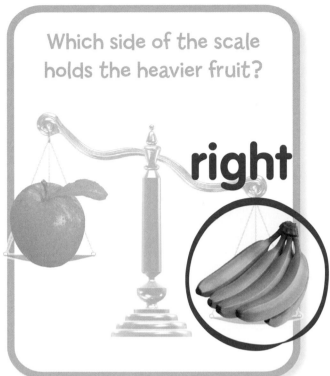

Which of these objects begin with the letter T?

turtle

train

Which two animals rhyme?

dog

frog

How many tops are there?

7

Answers for page 50

Which helper prepares food?

chef

How many tigers are there?

3

Do you see the letter **Z** hidden in the picture 7 times?

10

How many helicopters are there?

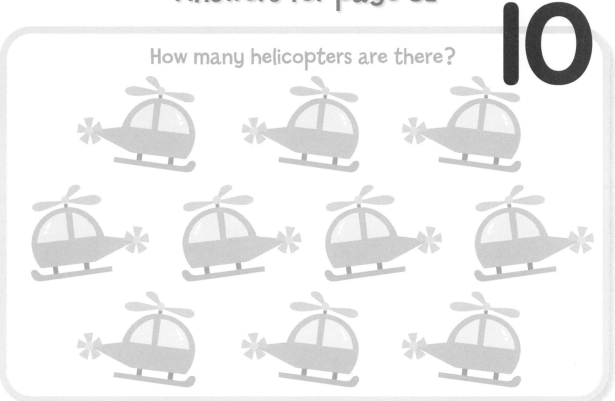

Which one is made from wool?

scarf

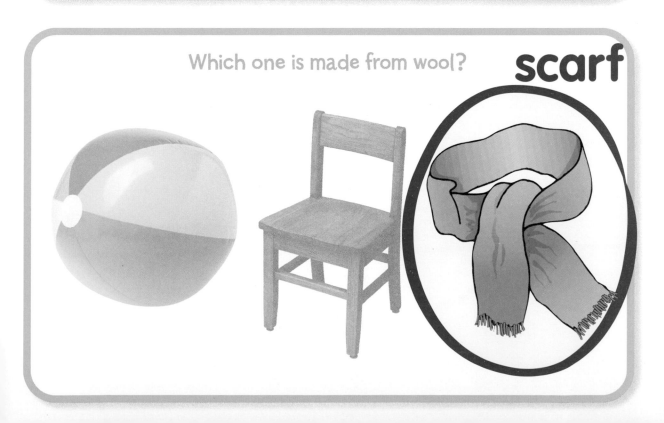

Answers for page 52

Which one is the dog?

Which two objects rhyme?

shake

cake

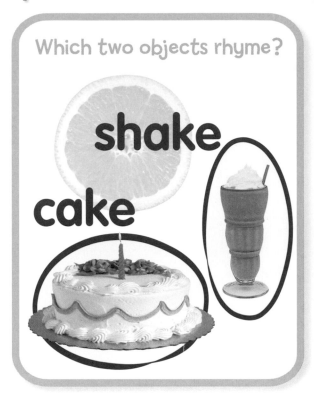

Which picture matches the word?

jar

Which one will stick to the magnet?

key

How many objects start with the letter **J?** 2

jacket

jeans

What is the correct order for these pictures?

2

1

3

Answers for page 54

Which person has blue eyes?

How many quails do you see? **6**

Which person helps you find books?

librarian

Which two objects rhyme?

clock
sock

Do you see the letter **F** hidden in the picture 6 times?

Look at the candles. How old is Puppy?

3

How many circles can you find in this scene?

8

Which picture matches the word?

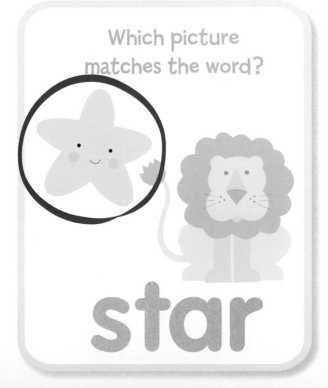

star

Answer for page 56

Find all the things that start with the letter y.

yarn
yo-yo
YOGURT
CHERRY
WITH OTHER NATURAL FLAVORS
yogurt

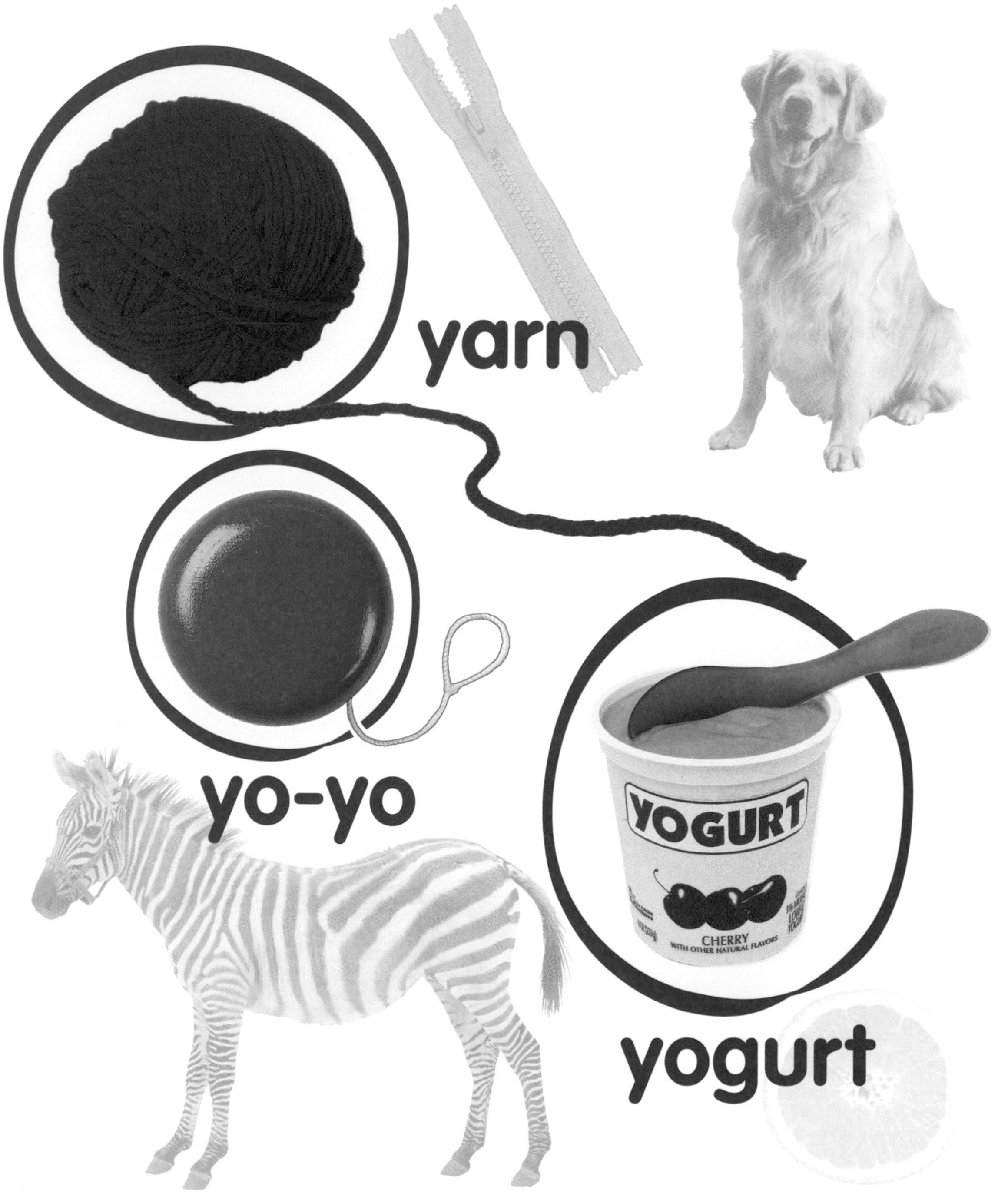

Do you see the letter **S** hidden in the picture 5 times?

Which animal lives in the nest?

bird

How many animals have spots?

2

Answers for page 58

Do you see the letter **W** hidden in the picture 4 times?

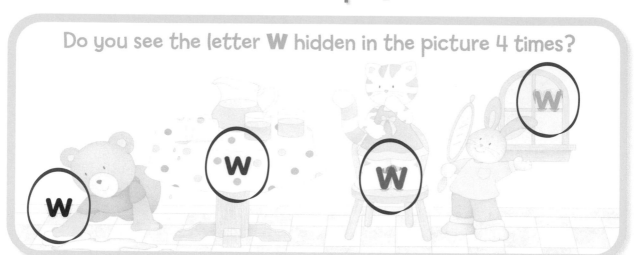

Which child is not following the rules?

He did not stop.

Which animal is exactly the same as the one in the circle?

How many rectangles do you see in the house?

6

Which ball is the same as the one in the square?

Which picture matches the word?

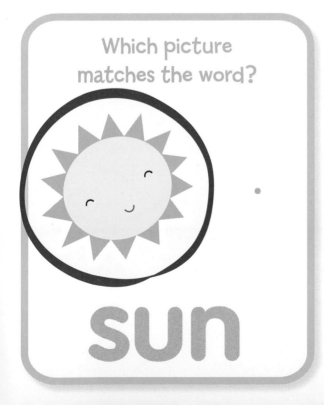

sun

What color button comes next?

blue

Answers for page 60

Which sea creature's name starts the same way as "jack"?

jellyfish

Which picture matches the word?

truck

Which creature made this web?

spider

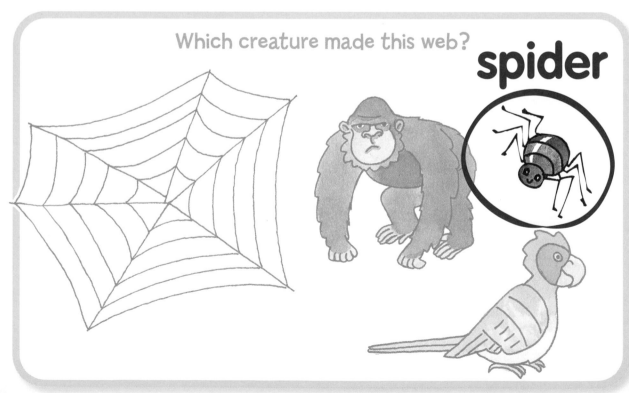

Which picture matches the word?

horse

Point to Earth.

Which of these is different?

How many monkeys are jumping on the bed?

Answers for page 62

What color gift comes next?

yellow

Uh-oh! Hippo knocked the plant over. What should he say?

Thank you.

I'm sorry.

Which of these starts the same way as "bat"?

butterfly

What is the correct first letter for this word?

fish

How many red wagons are there?

3

Which picture matches the word?

lamb

Which animal can live in cold places?

penguin

Answers for page 64

Which food should the rabbit eat?

carrot

What is the correct first letter for this word?

dog

Which one would you most likely see at Thanksgiving?

turkey

Which of these is different?

Which picture matches the word?

dinosaur

How many green trucks are there?

5

Which one would a baker wear?

What is the correct first letter for this word?

pig

Answers for page 66

Which one means "friend" in Spanish?

amigo

el gato

Which word starts the same way as "door"?

duck

Find the things that start with the letter **R**.

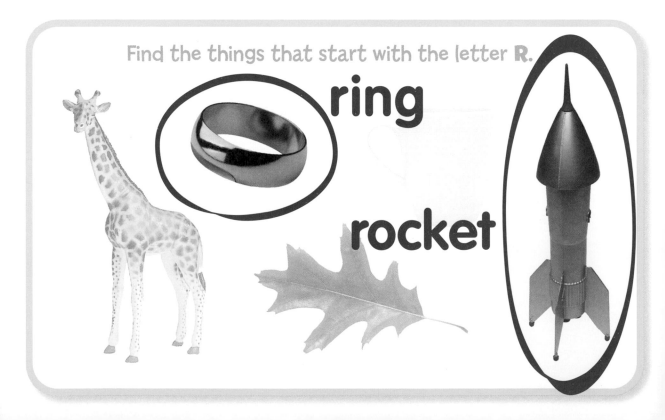

ring

rocket

Which picture starts the same way as "sun"?

sailboat

Point to the American flag.

Which of these goes with the brush in the circle?

Answers for page 68

Which picture starts the same way as "egg"?

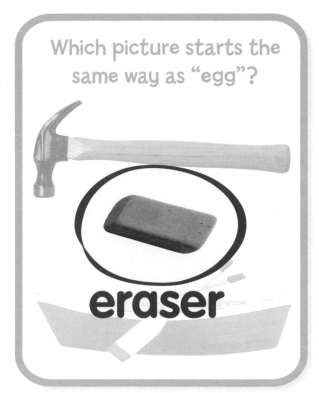

eraser

What do you brush before you go to bed?

teeth

Do you see the letter **X** hidden in the picture 5 times?

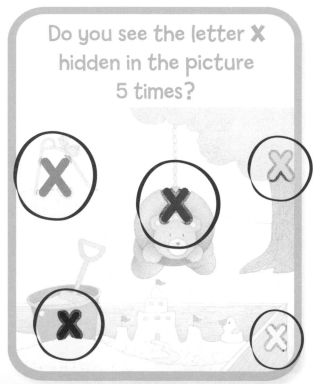

Which one means "stop"?

Which word starts the same way as "rock"?

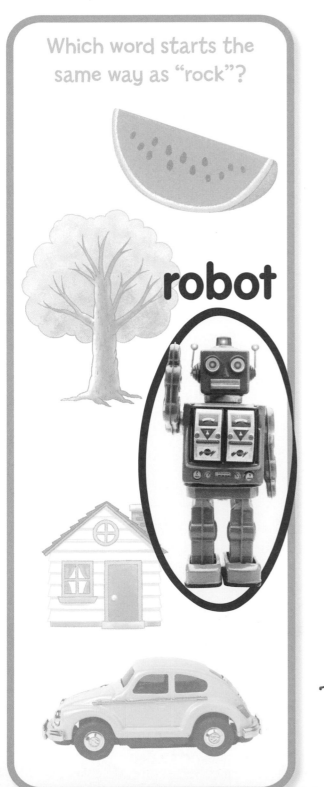

robot

Find all the things that start with the letter W.

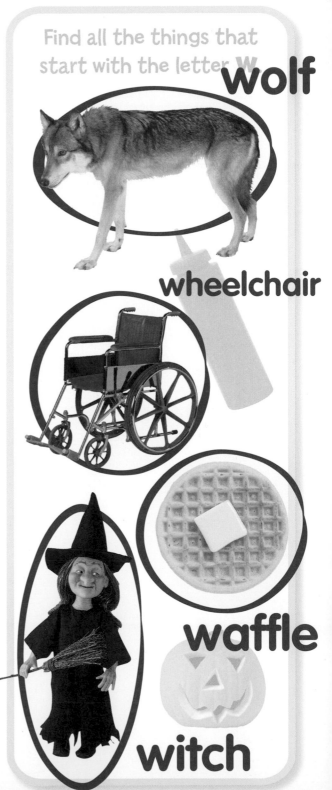

wolf

wheelchair

waffle

witch

Answer for page 70

6

How many yellow dogs are there?

Is the hat **on** or off the dog's head?

In this line, who is the closest to the teacher?

What's wrong with this picture?

Answers for page 72

Which drink is cold?

Which letter is a vowel?

Z
N **E**

Which one do you see at night?

moon

Which one means "thank you" in Spanish?

gracias

adiós

Point to the part of the face you use to smell.

nose

Which ball is the big one?

Find all the things that start with the letter **L**.

ladder

lamp

lion

lettuce

Answers for page 74

How many squares
are there?

7

What is the duck riding?

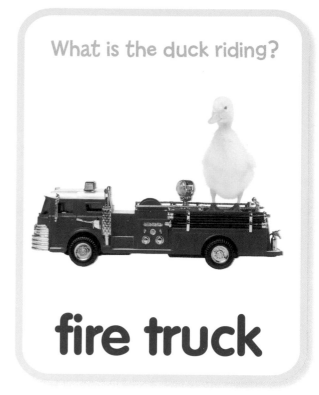

fire truck

Which person is a girl?

Which thing starts the
same way as "nut"?

nest

What is the clown wearing on his head?

crown

Which thing starts the same way as "igloo"?

ice-cream cone

How many diamonds are there?

3

Which animal has horns?

cow

Answers for page 76

Which animal lives here?

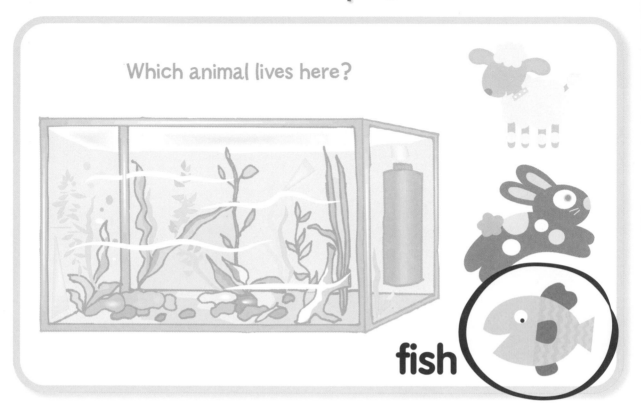

fish

Find all the things that start with the letter **S**.

shark

snowman

saxophone

Saturn

What's sitting
on the dog?

frog

How many yellow
stars are in the sky?

10

These letters are all mixed up!
Point to the letters in each
set in the correct order.

Answers for page 78

What is the correct order for these pictures?

2

3

1

What animal is in the boat?

alligator

goat

cat

Which of these is different?

Which person is jumping the rope?

Point to the part of the face you use to taste.

tongue

What color bead comes next on the necklace?

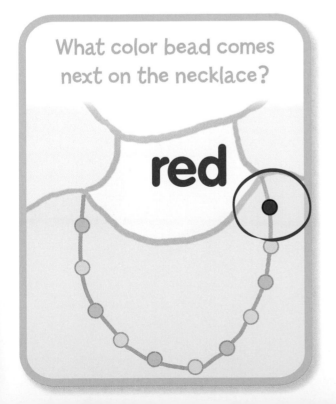

red

Which one is the farmer?

Answers for page 80

What kind of weather do you need an umbrella for?

rain

Which group of coins is equal to the exact price?

4¢

Point to the easel.

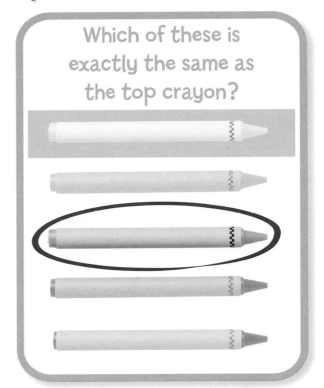

Which of these is exactly the same as the top crayon?

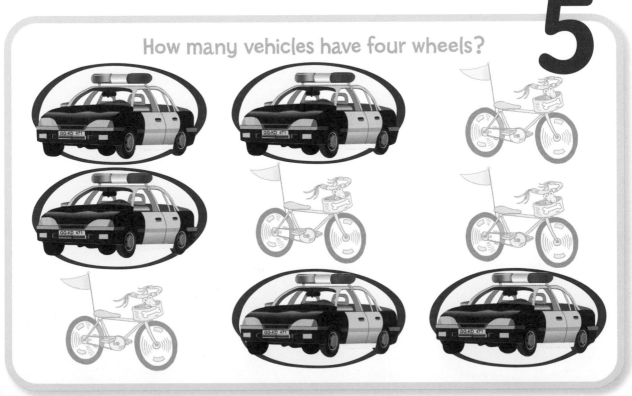

How many vehicles have four wheels?

5

Answers for page 82

Which is the oldest?

Which picture matches the word?

frog

Which bowl is the opposite of full?

empty

How many candles have stripes?

3

Which one is Little Miss Muffet?

What do you call a group of people who are all related? Here's a hint: It starts with the letter **F**.

family

Which one is floating?

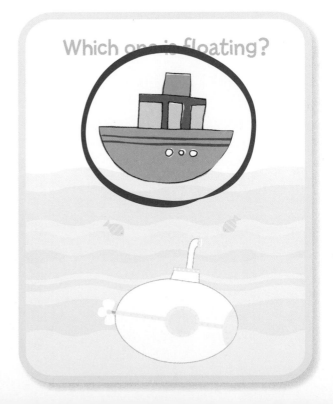

Answers for page 84

Find the word "stop" in this picture.

How many of these foods are fruits?

3

apple

orange

bananas

Answer for page 85

How many roller coaster cars are yellow?

Answers for page 86

Which letter is
a consonant?

Are there more **orange**
or pink dinosaurs?

Which person is
the mother?

How many dimes
are there? **8**

Are there more ducks or **ducklings?**

How many apples are red?

4

Which two things go together?

pencil

notebooks

What do you say when someone gives you a present?

Thank you.

Answers for page 88

What numbers would you dial in an emergency?

9-1-1

Which would you use to dance?

ballet slippers

Which animal is upside down?

pig

Answers for page 89

Which fruit has two sides that are almost exactly alike?

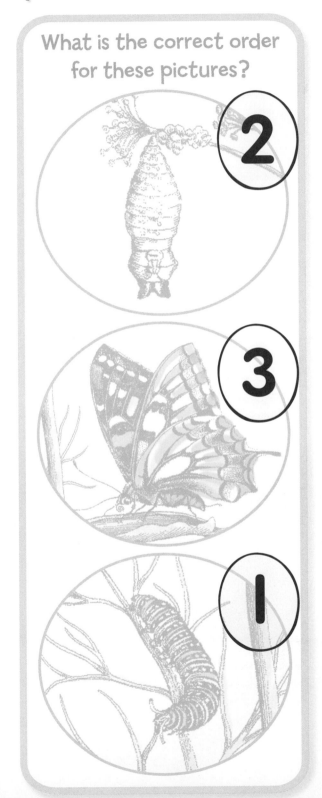

What is the correct order for these pictures?

2

3

1

184

Answers for page 90

Which one means
"good night" in Spanish?

buenas noches

estrella

Who sat on a wall and
had a great fall?

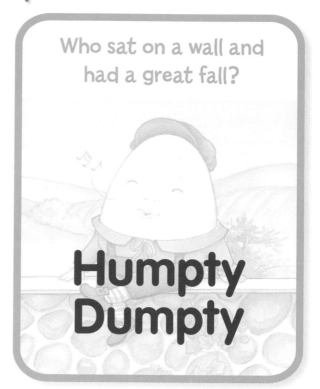

Humpty Dumpty

Which two things go together?

basketball

hoop

What is the correct order for these pictures?

3

2

1

Which one is on the bottom?

snail

Which person is the son?

Answers for page 92

Find the word "go"
in the picture.

Point to the bin you'd
use to recycle this
plastic bottle.

Look out the window.
Is the weather **rainy**,
sunny, or snowy?

What do you think the
mouse is doing?

singing

How many shirts have polka dots?

2

Who lives in the igloo?

Eskimo

Who is oldest?

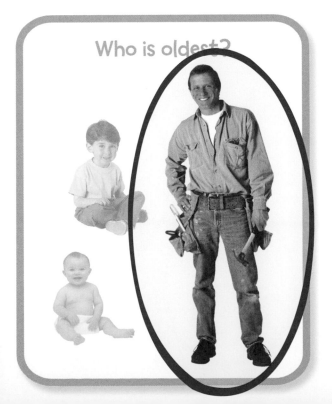

Which children are skipping?

Answers for page 94

What is the correct order for these pictures?

 **2**  **3**  **1**

Point to the chopsticks

Which group of coins is equal to the exact price?

 11¢

Point to the mouse.

How many things are hot?

2

soup

fire

Which two things go together?

dog

bone

What do you wash after using the bathroom?

hands

Answers for page 96

Find the word "ice" in this picture.

What do you say when you politely ask for something?

Give me

Please

How many nickels are there?

What kind of animal is
hiding on the tree branch?

chameleon

Find the word "bus"
in this picture.

SCHOOL BUS

How many pennies
are there?

7

What does a
helmet protect?

head